THE OTHER MERLION
AND FRIENDS

All illustrations by the poet.

Published by
Landmark Books Pte Ltd
5001 Beach Road
#02-73/74
Singapore 199588

Landmark Books is an imprint of
Landmark Books Pte Ltd

ISBN 978-981-4189-63-7
Printed in Singapore

THE OTHER MERLION AND FRIENDS

Gwee Li Sui

⋄LANDM△RK⋄BOOKS⋄

CONTENTS

This is for you,
All you bothersome people
Who ask about my next book,
Ask whether I still draw
Or write anymore.
What is my next book about?
When is it coming out?
When poets become rabbits,
You will get my next book.
Since you're now stuck waiting,
Do spare me the pained look:
There's more yet to learn.
When I am not writing,
I am not constipating.
That bowl of kway teow?
It is a bowl of kway teow,
Not some swirl of metaphors.
I don't see bobbing symbols,
I don't hear iambs or trochees.
What's wrong with you people?
This is for you.

CHARLOTTE UNBOUND

Mr and Mrs Lim used to read well-loved classics
To little Charlotte to sow the seeds of aesthetics.
At five, she would fly to the Literature section
Of a library and soon – to great expectation –
She was reading the poets, some verses from each one.
Meanwhile, her teacher saw a different trend begun
And called her parents down to show how she was spelling
April with two Ls, *tiger* with a Y, then ending
Lines with dashes, would not use a capital letter...
So they stopped her nonsense, got her a piano teacher
For there was not just no future in Literature,
It was also mangling her English.

A for egg
Beefor lamb?
C for yourself
D for thyself
E for some reason, you get
        F for effort
G for Jesus
H for onour
        it's I for an eye
J for gerrymandering
K if you don't mind
L for 'ello,
        M for God
                N for country!
O for heaven's sake
        P 'fore you go out
Q for what?
R for Arthur
        and S for Esther
T for the lady

Uforia

V heißt du?
Double U make me see
X for ecstasy
        but Y fall in love?
Zee for Xerox
        only in America –
                otherwise, Zed is all.

CONFUCIUS!

Confucius! Thou shouldst be living at this hour:
Thy folks have need of thee! They have become
All bureaucrats: pens, forms, letters, tiresome
Ping-pong matters – O how our old men cower
To one corner and wet their Eisenhower
Trousers! Are we no more than this feared sum?
Then raise again thy cane and beat us mum;
Teach us good sense, manners not to overpower!
For thou alone art most qualified and smart:
Thou art the poster boy of this strange age
That sees in paperwork a privilege.
So mock us: in the name of Ancient China,
Save us from more red tape and its counterpart –
Even more circulars blowing its tuba!

The Fate of Singaporean Poultry

Someone says we are killing poets now
and I jump, both feet pointing to the door.
"Must kill them, ya? They dangerous because
the bird flew!"
      Those words sweat me even more.
Poets are being lynched for some lost bird?
"He means poults," a voice bends close to retrace.
"They are culling five thousand at the farms
just in case."
      Just in case what? "Just in case"
should never be used to end sentences
like, you know... whatever.
            "Why, just in case
we get a case!" comes the reply. "We can't
know how every chicken feels at a place –
so, if even one rogue is suspected,
we must slaughter all two million on cue!
This measure, then, is but a practice run
to check our response to a grave issue,
to try our haste, keenness, resolution,
competence –"
      And our conscience, I advise.
"Yes, to a degree –"
      To *that* degree, no!
What we fail to do is to humanise
with a crisis. If this is a mere trial,
not the real thing, can't the deaths be virtual?

Can't we act as though we have culled? Why fix
a quick end to creatures whose medical
downfall hasn't arrived, might not even?
Besides, as there is no contagion yet,
every drill of this sort will always prove
a success. We are rehearsing to get
a piece of horror fiction defeated –
never mind the tied-in moral effect.
But, if our plan is never to negate
a threat, only to test speed and correct
procedures, then we surely needn't use
good chickens or they needn't be dead or
it needn't take five thousand – or we might
as well say the flu *did* hit Singapore
and five thousand chickens had to be killed!
Why make it so difficult to love life
in a premise? Turn it round: would we butcher
real people to simulate civil strife?

"All this you say," the cool voice jabs, "while you
gorge away on chicken rice?"
                                    I startle,

look down to see a broad slice of the bird,
steamed white and succulent as a bubble,
still pinned to my fork.

"It seems that, despite
what you say, your appetite understands
better how chickens and humans are not
the same –"

That's right!" the other voice now blends
in his terror. "Chickens and humans not
the same! You a poult, not a poet! See
this poetry we must kill and kill, poultry
we care less!"

Pavlov-trained, I jump to flee.

LOVE THY NEIGHBOUR FROM HELL

Hello? Police? I think my neighbour has SARS!
Her husband has hidden her at her Ah Ma's!
If you can give me her name
And the place where she works,
I'll let everyone know from here up to Tuas!

Hello? Police? My other neighbour is sick!
She has been too quiet for over a week!
I just caught a strange whiff
And, if she really is dead,
Will she happen to smell like barbecued steak?

Hello? Police? My downstairs neighbour, he said
I snore as loud as a Japanese air raid!
When you're free some time later,
Will you go let him know
He can knock on my door to see who's afraid!

City Life

I must really keep still,
I must stand in my stead
Because there is a city
On the top of my head!

Its dwellers are many
And they run to and fro
On the streets on my head
With few places to go!

Their lives are so fragile
I must really be mild:
God knows what will happen
If I should turn wild!

If I should breathe loudly,
They will surely go deaf.
They will all suffocate
Should I work as a chef.

I used to like TV,
But its rays are too strong
And sleep is a pleasure
That is morally wrong.

I have given up shampoo,
I have broken my comb,
I have cut out a corner
As a vertical tomb.

If some should keep living,
Some must sometimes seem dead.
So I stand stiff, mute and blue
For the city
           on the top of my head!

Godly Advice
(For the Kings and Queens of the Future)

Children,
    beware of adults!
Beware of those who will cock a snook,
tell you they know what life is about
because they really don't –
    nobody does!

Yet some will tell you not to turn right
because they've only gone left,
not to blow a snot bubble
with fish
    swimming in their breath!

Children,
    don't listen to them!
Turn up the music!
    Double spread your jam!
Follow your crayon line!
    Believe in monsters,
        feel the spring in your heels!
There's time enough to grow up,
    I feel.

Listen to nobody
        (except me)
or rather be your own adult,

wag a fat finger at yourself and shout
    "YOU LISTEN TO NOBODY!"

    And who knows?
With enough practice,
you might never need to grow.

An Introduction to Hesitation

You say Life is not black and white,
You say it knows no wrong or right.
That may be so, but I live each day
In dark and lighter shades of grey.

ONE-DISH WONDER

I must say that your thosai
is really damn shiok!
Your murtabak
and your briyani
I would rather not say...
So let's talk about your thosai –
it's really damn shiok!

Murruval or masala,
ghee, onion or plain,
I can eat your thosai
every day again and again!
But your chapati
and your prata
taste somewhat salah...
so let's just talk about your thosai –
it's really damn shiok!

THE SHORTER BOOK OF JOB

Poor old God!
They shouldn't have –
While His long beard twirls
Around His staff –
Been awfully keen
To say that He's mean
For, given His plan,
They just shouldn't have.

SAILING TO BYZANTIUM

I

Someone's grandfather got lost this morning.
He lives in a colour-coded building
              on the second floor.
              That and furthermore:
he commands the Queen's English, not the kind
with *lah*s and *lor*s I hear his children speak.
I believe they visit him every week
and bring with them good food. Today they find
that he has returned without returning.

II

"This can't be a country fit for old men!
The green light flashes way too soon and then
              we'd better run.
              If it could be done,
I might spend my days on buses in sleep!
My friends who are undead clean tabletops
while I haunt streets, void-decks and coffee shops,
circling invisibilities. Why keep
going when there is no one to listen?"

III

"One day, when I leave, don't come look for me.
I will have begun my Yeatsian journey
              to find Byzantium.
              These long years' tedium

will fade there upon the golden pavements
of my memories. The shimmering kids
will play once again in fields of orchids
while the old laugh loud, thoughtless of ailments.
All our voices, strengthened, will ring out free."

IV

After he did not return till he did
between two policemen, I go to bid
            him a late farewell.
            From what I can tell,
it isn't him behind the rusty gate.
This guy who eats porridge raised to his lips
has vacant eyes staring like an eclipse.
He sits unstirred by the noise we would hate
that pounds our sky daily into a grid.

A World of Difference

His charity
Is in the crumbs
He gives his mum
Just as his mum's
Is in the crumbs
She gives her pets –
Get that?

His affection
Lies in his mum,
Lies in the sum
Of all her pets
She finds to love
To feed with crumbs –
Get *that*?

THREE-WORD SUTRA

Gahmens at first
Are always good.
All their policies
Can be understood.

With time, complacent,
Their hearts recede,
So our votes
Start growing feet.

But, where there
Exists no contest,
Don't panic yet!
Don't go protest!

Lay low longer:
Someone should come
Who's either smarter
Or more dumb.

Wasn't PAP once
Able to please
As citizens rejoiced
To make babies?

But progress with
Family emerged rough,
So it mandated:
"Two is enough."

Now we've become
All bedroom bores –
Lacking babies, it
Throws open doors!

Our population explodes,
The economy booms,
Living costs soar,
Train breakdown looms...

Education had been
Oodles of fun
Before this hysterics
Over Number One.

From universities down,
The obsession grows.
Whether knowledge is
Loved, nobody knows.

With childhood scorched,
We're taken aback
That children are
Encouraged to slack!

Which parents would
Volunteer their kid?
Who would want
Theirs graded stupid?

Or consider how,
In its privilege,
Our gahmen has
Kept discourse underage.

With culture.little
And attachment less,
It resorts to
Promote more openness.

Then protesters throng
Hong Lim Park!
Online vigilantes grow
And ranters bark!

Unable to cope,
The grip re-tightens –
What is achieved
When authority frightens?

O the chimeras
We shouldn't ride!
O low-hanging fruits
We shouldn't bite!

O the ponies
We must kick
For having overperformed
One lame trick!

Only by routing
Those entrenching mess
Can society begin
To make progress.

But politics is
A funny game:
Who votes difference
Gets the same.

CHINESE WHISPERS

Well, it so happens –
Or so I have heard –
Quek met a woman
And she has a beard.

    She has a moustache
    She ties round her neck.
    It catches big flies
    They sell in a steck.

        There are ten flavours,
        But crunchy is best.
        The doctors say these
        Can cure with a rest

Flu, rheumatism,
Migraine, stinky breath,
Itchy ass, typhoid,
Syphilis and death.

Filzah hails them as
A breakthrough – you see,
Her mum is with the
Nobel committee!

Now the country is
A world research hub.
There is even a
Rocket in Siglub!

I hear Bilveer will
Be sent to the moon.
They bade him "So long!"
Just this afternoon!

So we're all getting
A fat raise this year!
The news is ablaze
And every bit suear!

The Leviathan

Mysterious is the world under its belly as its swims.
The sea of opinions parts from its ginomousness,
leaving many without homes. Soon, out of sunken daydreams,
the monster will stir and rise to foamier surfaces.
Never mind that its farts can blow whole islands off the world!
Never mind that its breaths deplete oxygen for weeks!
So long as we do not hear its voice that has unfurled
frightful nonsense before – but it's now too late. It speaks:

Be quiet and be still so as to be quieter!
I alone speak for – nay, as – the Silent Majority!
I, just me, in this glorious body, the approved breaker
of our monastic vow of silence and reverie!
I, now broker for your right to speak or to be quiet!
I, the chosen one, chosen by me since I choose to choose!
I, the thin and long snake of words on a diet,
ready to strike and harm if bothered back into use!

Do not mock me or ask how it is that I am not
as silent as I should be. All you scoundrels who do so
are in direct contravention of my sacred lot!
The rule of my exception defines my modest ego.
I as Supreme Voice of the Silent Majority
am surplus to the whole! I answer solely to those
who do not doubt my essential being, do not rouse me
out of me and then ridicule the reason I rose!

O I know you with your intolerable nest of sounds,
you the noisy minority with your blah-blah-blah!
You hammer cacophonies and shape them into grounds
to show that you are indeed greater than an iota.
Do you think that minds are swayed by your mimick-speech?
Do you imagine that you can ever out-preach me
when I can prove loudly my influence beyond your reach?
Hear my vacuous roar! Fear us Silent Majority!

MR FLEEGEE

Mr Fleegee has two eyes
And one of them is blind;
The other one is born impressed
Above his pale behind.

So like the fabled System
With no clue where it is going,
He always knows precisely when
His underwear is showing.

National Beverages

They invite me to tea
They say it starts at eight
"You're the *crème de la crème*
And this is *la drème* –
You'd better not come late!"

Then they call me for kopi
I wish to say "No thanks"
They say, "We have a brew
That is missing you –
So don't you pull any pranks!"

SONG OF INNOCENCE AND EXPERIENCE

My life has been a rattling coop
Till someone puts me in the loop.
Its round of sounds
Where faith rebounds
Restores my belief in the group.

Someone drops me from the loop.
This older silence after whoop
Has brought me fun
Enough for one.
I hold a melted ice-cream scoop.

Bookshop Fascism

They won't stock our books
They give us dirty looks
When we thumb through their shelves
They say "Don't do it yourselves"
(They have wrapped up their books)
They imagine us crooks
They say we're spine-benders
We destroy the crisp covers
We don't really read
If there were this need
We'd sprawl on their floor
We'd only read more –
"We have a business to run" –
They have a business to run
So with polythene sound
We turn each book round
(Or round) – they wonder why
They can't get us to buy
Perhaps we really are crooks
Perhaps they should block out the books
Put a band in the middle
Get a dance troupe to jiggle
Kick up some wild brawl
(Now you're welcome to sprawl)
If we're all weaned from reading
They may get down to selling
But they don't carry *our* books

"What? Those gobbledygooks?"
They say their main database
Shows no intelligent trace
They claim we hallucinate
Or at best overrate
What others abandon –
"You've *got* to follow the canon" –
What publishers publish
Is a truckload of rubbish
Every good reader knows
A really good author shows
By hardly getting a tint
What then gets to see print
Should be sieved for the shelves
(By them Samaritan elves)
They police free publishers
Policing free authors
And keep it all spinning
They keep us purchasing
To help them overlook
That oracular book
We know someone wrote it
And someone released it
Yet nobody stocks it
We should appreciate it
They're keeping us in touch
"You shouldn't be reading *this* much"
We eye them smothering a sneer
They're wishing their friends here
They're swaying to the Duke

As we scour for some book
Conscious not to be found reading
Not to tear the shrink-wrapping
Better to wait for the review –
"Hey! We're still watching you!"

THE EDUCATION OF TAN J. A., PRUFROCK

Well, let's discuss then, you and I,
this text we did, late last evening, try
to read upon a bench table.
One of us should now be able!
I'm hoping for you to talk...
My notes got eaten by a yellow dog.

Guess it's time for some small feat!
I shall hide this face that faces meet
behind the hairdo of another.
While at it, I stop to wonder:
Do I care enough? Do I truly dare
to shift my buttocks upon the chair?

In the room, the daydreams come and go.
My tutor looks like Michelangelo.

I've heard all this rambling before.
I've measured my footsteps through the door
and, to that overwhelming question,
sought to scream my indigestion:
"Here's what I think! I'll tell you all!"
Just to hear: "That's not it – and you appal."

So I didn't read my *Hamlet*. School
is for shopping and tanning by the pool.
Once I graduate, I can always muse
deferential, feel glad to be of use,
act cute and a little ridiculous,
always bureaucratic, meticulous.

I grow bored... I grow bored...
I play with the reef knot on my trouser cord.

Do I dare nibble on a sandwich
and then a banana and a peach
since the bell won't ring for me?
Such is excitement in the realm of C.
I picture myself in scholastic gown
till an angry voice wakes me and I drown.

Goodbye, Academia!

I wonder whether our PM
on the White House line a-forging
close mutual ties and cajoling
ever gets called Mr Hsien Loong Lee
because I've got it bad from Jack and Sam.
We may be discussing Jacques Derrida
or Gayatri Spivak, et cetera –
and then I'm Li Gwee Sui or Sui Li Gwee!

So thank you, postcolonialism,
thank your deconstructuralists
and lesser psycho-critico-babblists
who vomit essay after essay.
You really care Zen zilch for the schism
between Amy Tan and Hwee Hwee Tan,
you cite our critic as Kah Choon Ban
and yet get right Galileo Galilei!

Well, the next time I hear someone
in past tense mock Fu Manchu days –
"Weren't they vile, Mr Sui?" he says –
I will help him to sing falsetto
in the mental distance he has none.
No thought arrives prejudice-free
and, if you'll pause to count to three,
I have a fat boot too for your Pomo!

THE IDIOMATIC IDIOT

First I got a foot in the door
By keeping a foot in both camps.

Soon I was shooting my mouth off
From both sides of the mouth.

Wrong-footed with a bad taste,
I found my heart in my mouth.

Then I stuck my foot in my mouth
And shot myself in the foot...

THE OTHER MERLION

Look at me – I am special too!
A slick yet-uncurried fish head
on the taut body of a king!
My eyes are globules of porridge goo,
but infinite myths can be made
for an action hero who, rising,
has no vain mane to flick or shampoo.
A sphinx traversing the vast seabed!
A land-loose kraken, terrifying!

But do these plebeians even notice?
Everyone is drawn more to my
incompetent brother than to me.
The fool had curled to hide a penis
none ever saw and petrify,
fancying the wrong Gorgon of three.
Now he embodies so much cheese.
Meanwhile, nobody cares if I die,
nobody writes poems to me.

Good Laws and Good People

Good laws don't
make good people,
but good people can make
good laws.

Good people who do so
do so because they think
that good laws make
good people,

which they don't.

In fact, good people
don't need good laws;
it is not-so-good people
who need them
and, yes,
need them more
than good people
need them.

But some not-so-good people
can make laws as good
as some good people can
although the good laws made
may not make them good.

But, if good laws don't
make good people
and they are not always made
by good people,

then why bother with
good laws
if not-so-good laws
serve as well
or, rather, as badly?

Good laws for both good
and not-so-good people
are bad laws for
making good ones.

On the other hand,
good laws for good people
and not-so-good ones
for not-so-good people
are all not-so-good laws
because it is
not-so-good people
who need good laws
more than good people
need them,

as I have said.

This does not mean,
nonetheless,

that good laws
for not-so-good people
and not-so-good ones
for good people
is a good idea

since some good people
under not-so-good laws
will be tempted to become
not-so-good people

(although this is
a good law
for making good laws
since with fewer good people
and eventually none at all,

there will be no more need
for not-so-good laws
with everyone living
under good laws alone).

It seems then that
not-so-good laws,
if given some time,
will become good laws,
but good people,
given time,
will strangely become
not-so-good ones.

So always remember:
if you want good laws,
don't expect to find
good people around for long
and, if you want good people,
perhaps you should not think
about good laws,
not-so-good ones
and how to make
either of them
altogether

because good laws
or not-so-good ones
do not make good people.

Noodles and Rice

Some like yong tao foo with noodles,
Some like it with rice.
If I care less about messy oodles,
I hold with those who favour noodles.
But if I want it with less spice,
To eat it with rice
Is also nice
And will suffice.

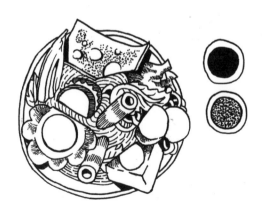

MIA

Makes you wonder –
makes *me* wonder –
where the books I wrote
are hiding now.
They packed their bags
and gave a bow;
in their free-fall,
they left like green bottles
from a wall.

Soon after,
I don't see them again.
They're not in the bargain corner
or those used bookstores
where other books retire.
When I snoop around the homes
of friends doing their chores,
I don't see them on their shelves
or in their drawers of underwear.
I don't find them in public libraries
unless I try really hard.
Once I was surprised
to discover a copy
miscategorised!

That must be it.
What are the chances
that elsewhere
they're filed between
kitchen appliances?

ODE TO THE MEMORY OF AH MENG

Ah Meng, she dead! Our nation's core is sunk!
Our childhood friend! Our favourite sister!
Our kindest matriarch swinging from trunk
to trunk – O how I already miss her!
She the spitting image of all our dads,
she the sweetheart who stole every first kiss,
whose thick lips, pleasured, would quiver and curl...
Was hers the face that launched a thousand ads
and left Prince Phil and Michael white with bliss?
Was there a hairier Singapore Gurl?

How, from Sumatra's wild jungles, she came
to our isle, shackled and unfree from birth!
She – but not her vile captors – was too tame
and, when enforcers saved her, sought to earth
her to Mandai, her boobs jiggled with glee.
Ah Meng, our entertainer from a raid,
worked hard for her day's comb of bananas.
She learnt much from Alagappasamee
and, with Bernard Harrison unafraid
to play Tarzan, the zoo became famoas!

So it was that she our Foreign Talent
grew into our choice First Lady. She our
illegal immigrant found employment
with the State – though detained to her last hour!
Ah Meng our rare durian-loving angmo,
our ambassador who was not travel-fit…
As mum, she failed to stop at two or three,
worse, let her kids run wild, swing to and fro!
As grand Monkey Mentor, she had her Mit
the People breakfasts regularlee!

O who recalls her mates or her children
Hsing Hsing (who migrated to Australia),
Medan, Hong Bao, Sayang, Satria even?
Who warms to that pretender Inuka?
Under cool daylight when she slipped away,
it was as though she just got on a bus.
Then the news spread. The day's 4D sold out.
A people's hopes fell into disarray.
All our best planning had not equipped us
for what life without Ah Meng was about.

SPECIAL OCCASION

MP is coming! MP is coming!
For weeks, the banners have been proclaiming
The flyers that miss the trash bins are saying
Now she's here and expects a welcoming
The grassroots leaders are smiling and pointing
Meanwhile, floor to floor, their helpers are running
But the doors are shut and people are hiding
Adults forbid their children from breathing
All that is heard is the knocking and screaming:
MP is coming! MP is coming!

THE SACKING

I've heard you shout, I've seen you flap,
You should have really shut your trap.
It gapes too wide,
To save my pride,
I need someone to take the rap.

Sanctum

What time is it
When the work piles up,
When you're eating your dinner
From out of a cup?
When the postcard picture
Has grass that looks greener?
When your hair is thinner
And your goldfish seems fitter?
O my friend,
You know you've been here –
It is time,
It is time
To disappear!

Surely it is time
To leave your inbox
And head to your doctor
To catch chicken pox!
Let your boss stretch his own dollar!
Let the phone pick itself up!
Do you need to be here
When the others crack up?
O my friend,
Your grand moment draws near –
It is time,
It is time
To disappear!

HAIR

She calls me a mess
So I'll leave my hair longer
To show her
What a mess looks like
So that the next time
She calls me a mess
At least we can agree.

OEDIPUS SIMPLEX

Who's the idiot who says
if you meet Buddha on the road
kill him?

If you meet Buddha on the road
leave him alone
don't kill anyone
and don't listen to stupid advice.

DEAR ASPIRING POET –

Fact is, you write bad poums.
Don't fault the doldrums
because others feel misery too
and their verses are beatifoo.

Call it professional ill,
call it what you will.
Be angry with me
if anger can help you be
the master of your grief.
Just don't feed your obese self-belief.
Writing on its own isn't magical.
What is, is to make it exceptional
with less rather than more.
Surely you've heard all this before?
If prose can express what hurts
with fewer or less showy wurts,
you're already in trouble.
Anything resembling a ramble
is a bucket hole that leeks.
This isn't what poetry seeks!

Then again – alass! –
you're of quite a different class.
You are all hole and no buckit!
Your verse throttles me to look at it
and I'm looking and I'm looking...
All I see is a Vast Nothing

in need of a tree to be sat under
for a very long time while you ponder:
Who am I? What the hell
am I doing to peopell?

Your poetry causes pain.
Please don't ask me to read it again
or I shall cry maniacally
as though a school bully
were beating up my soul.
Let's keep it all under controul
and you stop the hurting now.
Don't quote back to me on how
the garden of culture needs manure
manure.

The Specimen Bottle

So much depends on
So little that is achieved –
Who can be relieved?

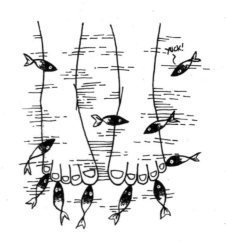

FISH SPA FISH

Nibble nibble
We think you are evil
For making us eat
From the flat of your feet
From the round of your toes –
They're hardly a rose!

The Cat-Woman

You will know her when you see her,
When you hear her come,
Her bags a-rustling –
The cat-woman!
A feline nearby leaves its fur.

She brings her bags of rice and meat,
Brings them here each night
In red plastic types.
The cat-woman's
Cats gather idly at her feet.

These guests don't care if she calls them
Or gets right who comes.
They convene to eat
The cat-woman's
Rice and meat – tonight, her steamed yam!

But whose food does she give away?
Who is she naming
And to whom she waves?
The cat-woman
Has been leading your thoughts astray.

She seems to thrive on cruel love.
The strays the humans
Ignore are nursed by
This cat-woman –
At least the ones who roam her turf.

You will know when she is leaving
When you hear her pack.
Scrunching a few bags,
The cat-woman
Consigns the rest to the evening.

Anonymity is the Best Friendship

You flamed me, I flamed you
We met at first on ICQ
We sparred in a forum and then a few
And played the racists that we knew
I became your stalker on IRC
And baited you for baiting me.

I spammed you, you spammed me
I sent an email times a hundred and three
You messaged "Get a penis enlarger free!"
And hid in MySpace to tee-hee-hee.
I hacked your Bebo to sabo you
For trolling me for trolling you.

You poked me, I poked you
We thought on Facebook to start anew
And then my friends – all two thousand and two –
Watched you trash my religious view
I cried "Infidel!", you screamed "Fundie!"
I screenshot you as you screenshot me.

I reported you, you reported me
We saw the police separately
And wailed about personal injury.
The police took us both into custody
To quiz us over and over who was who
Since you looked like me and I like you.

RACIAL HARMONY DAY

I ask what you're wearing
and you say baju kurung.
You ask what I'm wearing
and I say it's called changpao.
Raju walks by and we ask how
come he's in T-shirt and jeans.

Mid-Autumn Blues

My neighbour's boy
Burnt his lantern again.
He is shaping his mouth
Round as a moon
Except this one is
Dark, hollow and noisy.

THE UNSOLVED MYSTERY OF FRUIT FLIES

The doors are locked,
The windows are shut.
I take out a banana
And there it is.
Where the heck did this fella
Come from?

O look:
Here comes anotha.

RIME OF THE ANCIENT COFFEE SHOP REGULAR

The old beer-bellied man
With one hand on his beer
And the other on his belly
Calls me over:
        "Come here! Come here!"

My nosiness is swift
But my scruple too slow.
The moment I change tables
He sighs and begins:
        "Long ago,

"Before the Japanese came,
While the angmos were kings,
I was the handsomest man
For many miles:
          Little sweet things

"Girls from a dozen kampungs
Would make me. Thrilled somewhat,
Though the years were passing,
I told myself:
          Soon, Ah Huat,

"You must consider choosing
One damsel to whom you are man,
A daughter from just a few
Good families:
          It was then

"Also we became Syonan-to.
Parents mindful of lineage
Carted off my top choices
In quick blinks:
          Even in lost rage

"I had good muscles to keep
The virtue of maidens left.
There was a simple waitress,
A once-songstress:
          Her clumsy theft

"Locked her to the whims
Of young perverse soldiers.
Against eight of these I fought,
Fists before pistols:
          In time, tears

"Spurting from every bruised eye
Taught them fear for someone tough.
Twenty more awaited though
As chains snapped –":
          But this is enough.

Too long it takes me to learn
The old man is out of whack.
I leave him with two raised hands
Screaming:
          "Come back! Come back!"

To a Wisdom Tooth

Trooth is, the special filling didn't last.
By staying on, you were hurting my gums
all over again. For weeks, way past
my bedtime, I wept into my doldrums.
I thought of the good times we had munching
candies, crushing nuts, ice, bones, my sister's
rock cakes, and wounding bullies. Then something
felt awry when you brought out the daggers.
What could I do? So you were pinched away
before I thought to look you in the face.
When the cold steel dropped you, I saw little
of how deadly you seemed just yesterday.
Your assassin's cashier calls. In your space
of absence, I find that I can whistle.

The Visitor

Little mynah in my loo,
who through my little window flew:
will you make sure your every shot
is aimed into my toilet pot?

Will you regard my dinner mood
before you trample on my food?
Will you leave all my things alone,
go peck on barang of your own?

Little mynah, who through my loo
into my little studio flew:
when Hokkien words are all I spout,
it means it's high time you fly out.

ANNOTATION

Poetry the country
has many paths and many towns.
Its poets sometimes travel
to visit one another
and then pretend to reside
in that other domain
until, one night,
something wakes them,
calls them away again.

Here is a secret.
The poetry I write
aims to hide all of its action
from plain sight.
The game I play is invisibility.
The learned cannot care for it,
nor several poets.
It should be meaningless to review
and impossible to translate.
It cannot win me a single prize,
cannot have much general use.
These are my rules.
I must let Life do its job,
leave my readers to remember
the breeze in the bush.

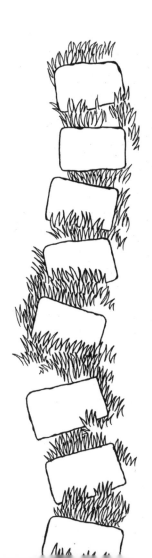

Many nights from now,
some who are seldom
at home in verse may realise
what it has only been about.
They will discover
behind the walls of my poetry
a secret path
and it will take them
on a long winding journey
through many towns and other paths,
into strange adventures.

I will be here at its end
where I have always been
and, when they arrive,
I shall part my arms and snigger
and say, Welcome.

So Long, Ah Kong...
and Thanks for All the Fish

You Da Man

You our father and our father's father and our father's
    father's father how that was even possible I dunno but
    you Da Man

You turned us from Swamp Thing to something a think-
    thing tinted and tinkered by a thinning Tintin whom
    we knew affectionately as you Da Man

You dragged da other men kicking and screaming out of
    jungles and sarongs and put them in homely hives and
    ironed workpants and through you our women
    became educated for which we are most thankful
    more thankful than you might actually be but
    you Da Man

You got us to shun yellow culture to cut our hair short
    not to speak dialects not to be corrupt to be courteous
    to stop at two to work to flush not to litter not to spit
    not to chew gum to work to save water electricity

money to work and we listened in every way because
you Da Man

You led us from Third World to First World like how my
Literature went from F9 to A1 in 1986 at a time when
we still feared becoming Second World which we little
knew was dying and so was Literature in schools since
it was da plan

You Da Man you da constant in every constituency that
has only known walk over and over and over because
no one dared to face your mighty party because they
understood too well how you Da Man

You da strongman and da wise man and da great man
and da noble man and da sweet man and da man with
da Kikkoman that made everything you cooked taste
so good and made us go O you Da Man

You Da Man scaring da angmos and da non-angmos and
da non-non-angmos everyone was in awe of you when
you said to jump we shouted how high and then
worked hard to afford foreign talents to do da jumping
for you Da Man

Da Man who stood at da far left end since all da rest had
to be right-hand men

Da Man at da top in all but housing where technically we
in modern flats live on da second floor and up

Da Man you and we loved you but we feared you and we
loved you but we also feared you and we dunno
anymore because you were larger than Life and Life
itself loved and feared you and said to you you Da Man
you Da Man you Da Man you Da Man you Da Man

Doing so for as long as it could until we took over and in
its place resoundingly proclaimed you Da Man!

SUBVERSIVE MESSAGE

Don't expect the world to wait for you!
As you nilly-nally, dilly-dally,
someone will sneakily push his cart
in front of you, steal your lover
who has kept her heart warm for you.

The secret is not to speed things up.
Rather, let those who must rush, rush.
They are nature's moving brooms.
They are dung beetles whose limbs must
spend time getting in front of time.

You put slowness into slowness.
Let time expand. Live between the ticks.
Stay still because under every footprint
is an everlasting kingdom where
the mind is clean and eyes are new,
where all the stuff you lost has never left.

WHAT RHYME OR REASON?

The day after you told me
About free admission
I took the day off
And tore myself
To the zoo.

There was no queue.
The gates were shut.
It was a weekday.
And the bus ride
Cost one-fifty.

LITERARY RAPTURE

Soon I will disappear.
Try as you may,
Hard as you look,
In a directory
Or the morning papers,
On the spine of a book,
You will not find me.
Cherish me now.

Soon I will disappear.
When my stature falls
And our scholars fail
And the powers in
Our well-oiled system
Get back on my trail,
You will not find me.
Remember me then.

LATE ADVICE TO YOUNG READERS

Never trust poets, I never do
They will slip a wrong-size foot into a shoe
They will talk too much if you yield a chance
Never trust poets: I don't, do you?

Acknowledgements

Funny poems aren't born to many poets. They groan out of a kind of imagination that betrays a kind of environment. I wish to express my love to the entire Gwee clan, whose endless riot of foibles and good humour has ruined me utterly.

Always I proclaim my eternal gratitude to Goh Eck Kheng of Landmark Books. His dogged passion for books as artefacts inspires me to squander away my productive years to put more garbage in his hands. Toji Cultural Centre in South Korea must also be thanked for those crucial months of peace in 2010, out of which came my first daydreams related to this book. More recently, Fun Toast has offered me a space to write with free flow of teh-O, for which I am ecstatic!

Two poems here appeared in another place before. "Confucius!" and "Oedipus Simplex" first saw print in *Mascara Literary Review* back in 2007. "The Shorter Book of Job" in this collection shouldn't be confused with another poem with the same title published in *Softblow Poetry Journal* in 2006. (Or should it?)

About the Poet

Don't let the title of this collection mislead you: Gwee Li Sui is a hermit. He grew up in the swamps of Toa Payoh, where he found the earliest victims of his wayward imagination. He draws comics and writes all kinds of poetry and prose, literary and academic, because he can. He used to be a university professor, but the depth and breadth of his learning terrified his former employers. Now he lives in a cave in the West. He can be spotted nightly crawling out to his neighbourhood kopitiam to dream under moonlight.